My Best Book of
Polar Animals

Christiane Gunzi

KINGFISHER

Created for Kingfisher Publications Plc
by Picthall & Gunzi Limited

Author and editor: Christiane Gunzi
Designer: Dominic Zwemmer
Consultant: Theresa Greenaway
Editorial assistance: Lauren Robertson
and Barnaby Harward
Illustrators: Michael Langham Rowe,
Robin Bouttell, Barry Croucher,
Brin Edwards, Rachel Lockwood,
Norman Arcott, John Butler, Chris
Forsey, John Francis, Alan Harris,
Linden Artists Ltd, William Oliver,
Bernard Robinson, Denis Ryan,
David Wright

KINGFISHER
Kingfisher Publications Plc,
New Penderel House,
283–288 High Holborn,
London WC1V 7HZ
www.kingfisherpub.com

First published by Kingfisher
Publications Plc 2002
First published in paperback 2003
10 9 8 7 6 5 4 3 2 1

1TR/0403/WKT/MA/128KMA

ISBN 0 7534 0748 5

Printed in China

Contents

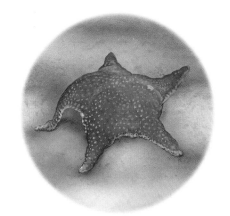

Frozen lands

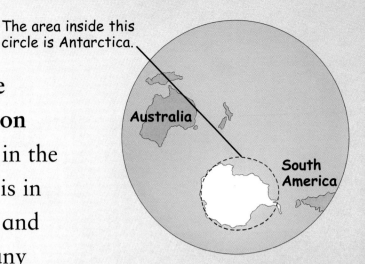

The area inside this circle is Antarctica.

Australia

South America

The polar regions are the wildest, windiest places on Earth. The North Pole is in the Arctic, and the South Pole is in Antarctica. These huge areas of snow and ice are bitterly cold and harsh, but many animals can survive there. Some leave during the coldest months of the year and return again in summer to breed. A few mammals, such as the polar bear and fox, stay in the Arctic all year round.

Antarctica

This is the coldest place on Earth, with huge icebergs, glaciers and mountains. In winter, the surrounding sea freezes into thick ice.

Surviving on a sea of ice

In winter, polar bears wander over the frozen Arctic pack ice searching for food. Arctic foxes often follow bears as they hunt for seals under the ice. The fox eats the bear's leftovers. It must not get too close though, in case the bear tries to eat it!

4

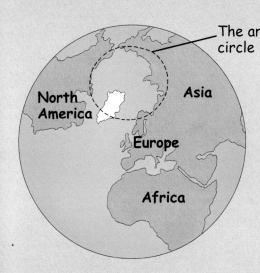

The area inside this circle is the Arctic.

North America

Asia

Europe

Africa

Musk oxen

Icy winds blow across the Arctic for most of the year. Musk oxen, polar bears, wolves and foxes can put up with this bad weather because their thick coats keep them warm.

Musk oxen huddle in a circle for warmth and protection

The Arctic

Much of the Arctic is a frozen desert. In winter, the great sea, called the Arctic Ocean, freezes over to form a huge blanket of ice.

5

Living in an icy world

The wolf is one of only a few mammals that live in the Arctic all year round.

Thick fur helps to protect this predator from the extreme cold. Wolves usually live in packs or in family groups. During the winter they are always on the move, hunting for prey. Arctic wolves can survive for days without eating any food.

Pale-coloured fur camouflages Arctic wolves as they hunt for prey around the icy Arctic.

Snowshoe hare

A snowshoe hare has large, furry pads on its feet to help it to grip as it runs over the snow and ice. In the winter, when the ground is covered with snow, a snowshoe hare's fur turns white. This camouflage helps it to hide from predators such as wolves.

Food for the pack

Arctic wolves mainly hunt large prey such as musk oxen and caribou. They also eat lemmings and hares. One musk ox is enough to feed a wolf pack for several days. Wolves sometimes travel up to 1,000km in search of prey.

Animals of the Arctic

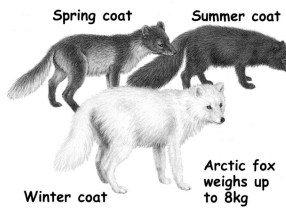

Spring coat   Summer coat

Winter coat   Arctic fox weighs up to 8kg

During the coldest months of the year, when the ocean freezes over, many animals leave the Arctic. Some spend the winter on the tundra and others migrate further south until spring. In summer, the sun shines all day and all night in the Arctic, and it melts the frozen sea ice. Many mammals and birds return at this time, to feed and breed during the short Arctic summer.

Keeping warm

Foxes, wolves, bears, seals and musk oxen have thick fur to keep them warm. In winter their coat is even thicker. The fur of Arctic foxes and hares changes colour to camouflage them.

Ringed seal up to 1.5m long

Harp seal up to 2.2m long

Beluga up to 5.5m long

Northern right whale up to 18m long

Little auk
up to 20cm high

Ptarmigan
up to 35.5cm high

Snowy owl
up to 65cm high

Ivory gull
up to 44cm high

Puffin
up to 30cm high

Moose
up to 2.3m high

Musk ox
up to 1.5m high

Polar bear
up to 1.6m high

Walrus
up to 3.7m long

Narwhal
up to 4.7m long

9

Animals of the Antarctic

The only mammals that live in the Antarctic are whales and seals. There are many kinds of seabirds, and the water is teeming with fish.

In winter, the sea surrounding Antarctica freezes over and the continent almost doubles in size. Many animals migrate to warmer areas, and return in the summer. The emperor penguin is one of the few animals that lives in Antarctica all year round.

Elephant seal
up to 6m long

Ross seal
up to 3m long

Leopard seal
up to 3.6m long

Fin whale
up to 26m long

Humpback whale
up to 16m long

Marble plunderfish
up to 30cm long

Adélie penguin
up to 71cm high

Black-browed
albatross
wingspan up
to 2.4m

Brown skua
up to 58cm high

Body warmers

Seals and whales have blubber
under their skin to protect them
in the icy water. Seabirds such as
penguins also have fat under the
skin, and layers of down and
feathers to keep out the cold.

Sheathbill
up to 43cm high

Emperor penguin
up to 1.1m high

Weddell seal
up to 2.6m long

Crocodile icefish
up to 75cm long

The tundra in summer

Around the Arctic there is a huge frozen plain called the tundra, where no trees grow. In winter it is dark for most of the time, and the temperature falls far below freezing. In summer the ice melts, and the tundra bursts into life with colourful flowers and insects. Grasses, mosses and lichens provide food for musk oxen and other plant eaters.

Snowy owl

Hunters of the tundra

The snowy owl hunts during the day for lemmings, voles and hares. It sometimes catches other birds too. Lynxes, wolves and foxes also hunt on the tundra.

Lynx

Cottongrass

Lichen

Arctic poppy

Ptarmigan

Caribou

Many mammals, such as lemmings, live on the tundra all year round. Caribou spend the winter in forests 1,000km further south. In summer, caribou return to the tundra in herds to breed and feed on the rich grass.

Caribou with calf

Dragonfly

Musk oxen

Purple saxifrage

Moss campion

Fritillary butterfly

Lemmings

The great sea bear

The polar bear is king of the Arctic. This mammal is an excellent swimmer, and its toes are partly webbed to help it paddle along in the water. The polar bear's pale, thick fur keeps it warm during the Arctic winter. Each hair is hollow, and the fur is not heavy when it is wet. The bear can swim for long distances without stopping.

Sneaking up on seals

A polar bear's favourite prey is seals. It can smell a seal up to a kilometre away and sometimes follows them for hundreds of kilometres. The polar bear usually sneaks up on the seals from behind. If they see a bear approaching, seals dive into the water and swim away.

Ringed seals keeping a lookout for polar bears

Polar bear swims with only its head poking out of the water

15

Snow babies

Male polar bears often spend the winter hunting on the sea ice. But the female settles down in a winter den on the side of a hill, far away from other bears. After about 60 days, one or two fluffy white cubs are born. The newborn cubs are tiny, but they grow fast because their mother's milk is very rich. The cubs usually stay with their mother for the first two years or so.

1 The tiny, newborn cubs are blind and helpless at first. They start to feed on their mother's milk straight away, and she washes them.

2 The mother bear does not eat anything all winter while she is caring for her cubs. She becomes very thin, but her cubs grow well.

3 In the spring, the female leads her cubs out of the den. She is very hungry and must hunt for food. The cubs will watch their mother hunt and begin to copy her.

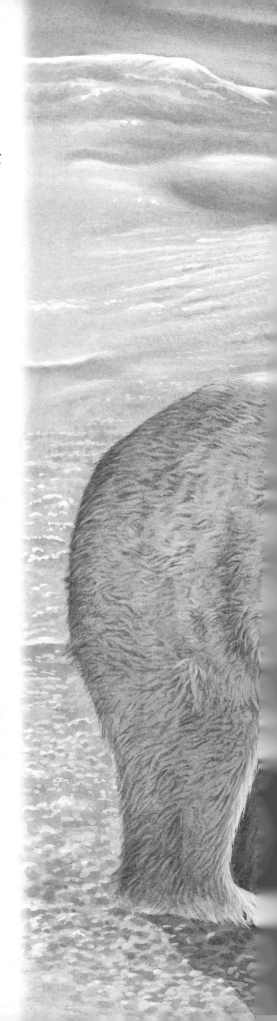

Caring for cubs

A female bear never lets her cubs stray far. She guards them carefully in case a large male tries to kill them. The male polar bear is much heavier than the female, and stronger too.

Female polar bear guarding her young cubs against a male

Polar fox

The Arctic fox is well suited to its frozen home. It has furry pads on each foot so it can run long distances over the cold snow and ice to hunt for food. Thick, fine fur keeps the fox warm, and at the coldest times of the year, the fox digs tunnels under the snow for shelter. Other animals find it difficult to spot this fox as it races across the snow in its white winter coat.

Ringed seal pup

Arctic hare

Ptarmigan

Shore crab

Barnacle
goose eggs

Berries

Vole

Changing colour

The fox's coat camouflages this mammal in summer and winter as it hunts for prey. In summer its coat is greyish-brown. This turns into a white coat for the icy winter.

Ground squirrel

Food for Arctic foxes

In summer, there is plenty of food for foxes, including ground squirrels, voles, birds and berries. Foxes bury a store of food in the summer and save it for winter.

18

Living on leftovers

Foxes are scavengers. In winter, when there is not much to eat, they depend on polar bears to catch their food. The fox eats the bear's leftovers. Later, gulls come along and eat what the fox has left. Nothing is wasted.

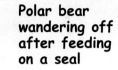

Polar bear wandering off after feeding on a seal

19

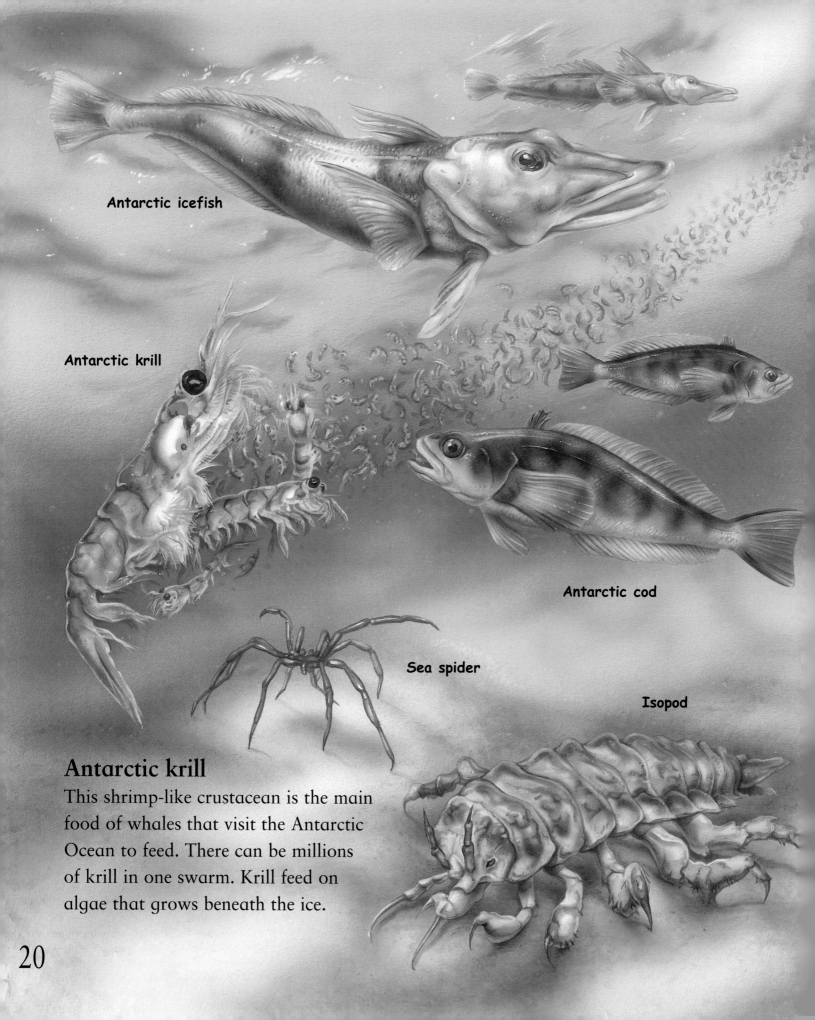

Antarctic icefish

Antarctic krill

Antarctic cod

Sea spider

Isopod

Antarctic krill

This shrimp-like crustacean is the main food of whales that visit the Antarctic Ocean to feed. There can be millions of krill in one swarm. Krill feed on algae that grows beneath the ice.

Deep under the ice

Jellyfish

Squid

Starfish

There are at least 200 kinds of fish living under the frozen sea ice of the Antarctic, but scientists know little about how they live. Most of these fish are types of cod and icefish. They have a special substance in their blood that stops their body freezing. As well as fish, many other kinds of animals are found in the seas around Antarctica, including squid, starfish, jellyfish, krill, seals and huge whales.

Migrating minke

The minke whale migrates to the Antarctic in summer to feed on the huge swarms of krill in the sea. This small baleen whale is one of the most common whales in the Antarctic.

Super swimmers

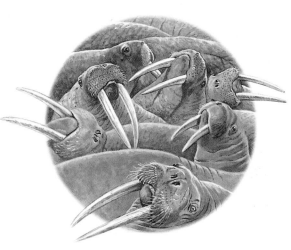

Walruses and seals have a thick layer of fat, or blubber, to keep them warm. These sea mammals spend much of their lives in the water, and swim using their flippers. Some can dive to great depths to find food, and hold their breath underwater for up to half an hour at a time. Seals hunt for fish, molluscs and crustaceans. Walruses use their long tusks to root about on the seabed, searching for clams and other molluscs.

Wandering walruses

Walruses live near the edge of the Arctic ice all year. In summer they swim further north to breed. Walruses are huge and heavy, but they are very good swimmers.

Adult harp seals hunting for fish in the Arctic Ocean

Leopard of the sea

The leopard seal is the fiercest predator in the Antarctic. It patrols the edge of the sea ice, waiting for penguins to dive into the water. Leopard seals also feed on krill, and they sometimes hunt other seals.

Leopard seal chasing an Adélie penguin

Harp seal pup on the ice

Harp seal

A harp seal pup feeds on its mother's milk for just 12 days. Then the female leaves it to look after itself. The pup's pale fur helps to camouflage it.

Flying in the waves

Penguins are perfectly suited to life in the water. These birds are clumsy on land, but in the ocean they are agile and graceful. A penguin's body is smooth and streamlined like a seal's, so it can glide through the waves with ease. Tough feathers and a thick layer of fat keep Antarctic penguins warm. Some of them live in huge groups called colonies.

Types of penguin

There are 17 types of penguin. The emperor, king, gentoo, rockhopper, chinstrap and Adélie live in Antarctica. The macaroni lives on islands that are close to Antarctica.

Emperor's new clothes

An emperor penguin chick is covered in fluffy down to protect it from cold winds. To keep warm, the chick stands on its parent's feet!

Emperor
up to 120cm

King
up to 90cm

Macaroni
up to 76cm

Chinstrap
up to 75cm

Gentoo
up to 75cm

Rockhopper
up to 63cm

Adélie penguins
walking to the sea
from their rookery

Taking a dip

Penguins are expert swimmers and divers,
and they seem to fly through the water.
They stay under for a few minutes, then
come up to the surface to breathe. Adélie
penguins sometimes swim more than
100km from the shore to feed on krill.

Penguins paddle with
their wings and steer
with their tail

All sorts of seabirds

Huge numbers of birds visit the polar regions, including gulls, terns, albatrosses and petrels.

Most of these seabirds make nests on islands, where they gather in large colonies. A few birds, such as emperor and Adélie penguins, breed on the continent of Antarctica itself. Seabirds feed on fish, squid, octopus and crustaceans. They glide above the ocean, then dive into the waves to grab their prey.

Arrows show tern's journey

Travels of the tern
Arctic terns breed in the Arctic in summer. When winter arrives, they fly to the Antarctic.

Blue-eyed shag

Grey-winged petrel

Arctic tern

South Georgia pipit

Wandering albatross
This huge seabird roams over the oceans searching for octopus, cuttlefish and squid. Its enormous wings measure about 3m from tip to tip.

Wandering albatross

Wilson's storm petrel

Ivory gull

Brown skua

27

Polar life in danger

People mine for coal and oil in the Arctic, which damages the wildlife there. Now many countries have agreed not to mine or drill for minerals in Antarctica for at least 40 years. This important agreement is called the Antarctic Treaty. If people start mining or drilling for oil in Antarctica, the animals there will be harmed. Antarctica is the only wild place on Earth that is not being damaged by humans. It is important not to pollute it.

Poisoned polar bears

The Arctic is being polluted by human rubbish. Polar bears, foxes and other animals wander over rubbish dumps that people use, searching for food. As the animals eat the scraps that they find, they are often injured by broken containers. The animals are also poisoned when they swallow harmful liquids such as chemicals.

Polar bear searching for scraps of food on a rubbish dump

28

An animal
rescuer cleaning
oil off the beach

Oil spills in the ocean

Huge ships that carry oil sometimes sink, leaking the oil into the oceans. Slicks form on the water and over beaches. When polar animals become covered in sticky oil they are not able to move around or breathe properly. They usually die if the oil is not removed.

Saving polar life

We must protect the Arctic and Antarctic so that animals living there, such as polar bears, seals, penguins and whales, can survive into the future. Many people believe that the polar areas should be made into huge nature reserves. This would mean that all polar animals would be able to live in their natural habitats without being disturbed by people.

Saving baby seals

To stop people killing seal pups for their beautiful white fur, a bright red dye is sprayed over their coat. The dye does not harm the pups, and fades after a while.

Chinstrap penguins being filmed in their Antarctic nesting site

Studying wildlife

Experts study animals in their natural habitat to find out how they live, and how to protect them in the wild.

Television crews film polar wildlife so that people can learn about animals without having to travel to the Poles.

Glossary

algae Simple plants, including seaweed and phytoplankton.

Antarctic The south polar region. This includes the continent of Antarctica and its oceans.

Arctic The ice-covered region around the North Pole.

baleen The huge, fringed plates inside the mouths of baleen whales such as the minke whale.

blubber The thick layer of fat beneath the skin of a whale, seal or walrus that keeps it warm.

calf A baby whale, deer, cow, dolphin or elephant.

camouflage The colours, patterns and markings on an animal that help it to hide in the wild.

carnivores Animals, such as seals, polar bears and wolves, that kill and eat other animals.

crustaceans Certain animals, such as krill, shrimps, lobsters and crabs, that have a hard outer covering. Most kinds of crustaceans live in the oceans.

glacier A river of ice that moves very slowly.

habitat An animal's habitat is its natural home. A penguin's habitat is the frozen land and cold seas of the Antarctic.

herd A large group of mammals, such as caribou or cattle, that live together.

iceberg A huge lump of ice that has broken off from a glacier or an ice shelf. Only a tiny part of the iceberg shows above the surface of the sea.

krill Shrimp-like crustaceans that live in the oceans in huge groups called swarms.

mammals Animals such as wolves that are covered with fur or hair, give birth to live young instead of laying eggs, and feed their young on milk.

migrate Animals migrate when they travel from one area to another to find food or to breed.

plankton Tiny creatures and plants that live in the sea.

predator An animal that hunts other animals.

prey Any creature that is killed and eaten by another animal.

rookery The home for a group, of penguins, walruses or seals.

scavenger An animal, such as an Arctic fox, that feeds on food left by other animals.

territory The area where an animal lives.

tundra The area of tree-less land between the most northern forests in the world and the ice surrounding the North Pole.

tusk An animal's tooth that grows very long.

Index